S U

Review & Analysis of
Treacy's Book

Double-Digit
Growth

—— BusinessNews Publishing ——

BOOK PRESENTATION: *DOUBLE-DIGIT GROWTH* BY MICHAEL TREACY

SUMMARY OF *DOUBLE-DIGIT GROWTH* (MICHAEL TREACY)

BOOK PRESENTATION: *DOUBLE-DIGIT GROWTH* BY MICHAEL TREACY

BOOK ABSTRACT

For any business, growth is like oxygen – it's essential. Growing companies thrive and attract all the best talent and resources whereas shrinking companies tend to wither and die. Smart managers understand that, and make certain their enterprises chalk up steady double-digit growth year after year irrespective of the state of the economy, the competitive pressures of the marketplace, the demands of customer and suppliers or any other considerations.

A study of 130 organizations that achieved double-digit growth year after year identified six key principles they adhered to:

1. They hedged their bets and spread the risk by pursuing multiple growth strategies, not just one or two.
2. They took small bites – and tried to achieve small gains in multiple areas rather than large gains in just one area.
3. They tried both organic and acquired growth strategies, and balanced these two approaches intelligently.
4. They were obsessive about offering customers a superior value proposition.

5. They created the management capacity to be able to manage growth projects without ignoring their existing business.
6. They put in place a corporate culture and internal processes which encouraged the achievement of growth.

So how, specifically, can a business achieve steady double-digit growth? The key factor isn't so much what industry you operate in as it is mastering and then balancing five key growth disciplines:

The five key disciplines of business growth

1. Keep the growth you already have.
2. Take the business away from your competitors
3. Position yourself where growth will happen
4. Invade your adjacent markets
5. Consistently invest in new lines of business

Balance

Have a balanced portfolio which contains growth intiatives in all five disciplines

In short, to achieve and sustain double-digit growth is a choice every business can make. Any company which applies the five disciplines systematically and consistently can and will achieve sustainable growth. The choice is yours.

"Double-digit growth is not a dream but a plausible scenario. If the challenge of double-digit growth appears a bit daunting, undaunt yourself and take heart. The beauty of the five growth disciplines is that any

company is capable of carrying them out, consistent with its own particular ambitions and circumstances."

– Michael Treacy

ABOUT THE AUTHOR

MICHAEL TREACY is a business consultant, management speaker and entrepreneur. Dr. Treacy (a graduate of the Massachusetts Institute of Technology and the University of Toronto) was previously a professor of management at MIT's school of management. He is the co-founder and chief strategist for GEN3 Partners, a business consulting firm specializing in product breakthroughs. Dr. Treacy's previous book, *The Discipline of Market Leaders*, was published in 1995 and was widely acclaimed as groundbreaking.

Dr. Treacy's Web site is at www.michaeltreacy.com.

IMPORTANT NOTE ABOUT THIS EBOOK

This is a summary and not a critique or a review of the book. It does not offer judgment or opinion on the content of the book. This summary may not be organized chapter-wise but is an overview of the main ideas, viewpoints and arguments from the book as a whole. This means that the organization of this summary is not a representation of the book.

SUMMARY OF *DOUBLE-DIGIT GROWTH* (MICHAEL TREACY)

GROWTH DISCIPLINE #1: KEEP THE GROWTH YOU ALREADY HAVE

One of the easiest and most direct ways to grow is to slow the rate at which you lose existing customers. Improve your client retention rate so you have a good base to build on. If your business provides good value-for-money, it will usually be easier to retain an existing customer than it is to attract a completely new customer.

It is generally accepted that it's easier and cheaper to retain an existing customer than it is to win a new customer. Yet despite that, very few businesses analyze what they have to do to retain their existing customers. In practice, there are three key principles of customer retention:

1. *Shape your customer's value criteria* – that is, find out why your customers chose to buy from you and give them more of what motivated them in the first place. You are better positioned to find out more about your customers than any of your competitors are. Use that inside knowledge to your advantage.

2. *Increase the cost of switching to someone else* – in terms of aggravation, inconvenience and direct costs. This is why many companies offer new customers

better deals than their existing, loyal customers can obtain. It may seem unfair, but it helps offset the costs of switching from one supplier to another.

3. *Narrow the customer's alternatives* — by embedding add-ons into the product or service bundle in such a way that it becomes difficult to compare one company's offerings with that of a competitor. When this is done effectively, the number of alternatives which are considered by the customer is reduced appreciably.

Applying these principles, there are four basic tactics organizations can use to increase their customer retention rates:

1. **Make your services sticky.**
   The objective here is to entangle customers with enough immediate added value that none of your competitors will be able to come up with an offer big enough to outweigh their switching costs. Usually, this involves adding in free services or educational programs but it may also include providing implementation expertise or other technology improvements.
   For example, GE Medical Systems sells complex medical equipment. To assist clients, GE Medical helps them manage the life cycle of their equipment by providing:

   ° Capital planning and financing.
   ° Ongoing performance monitoring and benchmarking.
   ° Regular maintenance and upgrades.

- Assistance with equipment disposal.
- Help with identifying revenue generation opportunities.
- Identification and execution of operational improvements.
- Fine-tuning of clinical service performance.
- Help to improve the clinical outcomes.
- Leadership development for program administrators.
- Help with management of clinical information.

Through these and other long-term initiatives, GE Medical Systems is attempting to align its own rewards with the success of its customers making it difficult (if not impossible) for any competitor to do likewise.

2. *Tailor your offerings.*

By using information about past purchases and preferences, a company can create a unique offering that the customer will not be able to find anywhere else. This will only work if you understand your customer's behaviors, motivations and value judgements intimately and in fine detail.

For example, Harrahs offers a loyalty card which gives customers rewards when they use it. This allows Harrahs to gather information about customer behaviors and preferences. They then turn this data into actionable insights by making customers offers they are predisposed to accept. The customer feels more "at home" and Harrah's has an opportunity to arrange future visits which build the business.

3. ***Preempt customer defections.***

For this tactic to work, companies must do three things right:

° Predict which customers are just getting ready to leave.
° Fashion an effective response.
° Execute that response to the customer's satisfaction.

At times, one part of your organization may know the customer is disgruntled. The tricky part is sharing that information with another part quickly enough to respond. This is often difficult to systemize effectively. For example, mortgage companies are famous for disregarding signals a customer is about to leave. When someone calls up and asks for a settlement figure for their mortgage, that's a pretty clear-cut signal they are considering a change. Yet very few mortgage companies pick up on that signal and have a salesperson call to see whether they can be of assistance in arranging their next mortgage or to offer other mortgage products.

4. ***Bond with customers.***

° Every purchase has a logical element and an emotional element. This is why brands are so useful – they convey what the seller stands for and what experience they aspire to deliver customers. Quite simply the deeper the emotional experience you can provide customers, the greater your chances are of doing more business with that person again in the future.

° The standout example of this customer retention tactic is Apple Computer. By rights, Apple has such a small market share that it should not be able to survive. Yet Apple does survive because it has created such an emotional bond with its customers that it is able to tenaciously hold on to them. Apple does this by enlisting everyone who buys one of its computers as active participants in a titanic struggle against the PC. Apple knows its customers very well and runs ads that not only entice new buyers but also reinforce the validity of its current customer's decisions.

"The growing level of customers' interest in superior value is a phenomenon of our time, and so is their growing skill at finding it. Luckily for business, however, most customers and companies are not ubershopers. Their decisions are shaped by all kinds of influences other than the quality and price of a product or service. They are still inefficient shoppers, and they are still susceptible to the base retention principles and strategies discussed. Were it otherwise, consistent double-digit growth would be even more difficult to come by."

– Michael Treacy

"When a customer leaves your company, it's like a tax on growth. Customer defections come right off the top line."

– Michael Treacy

GROWTH DISCIPLINE #2: TAKE BUSINESS AWAY FROM YOUR COMPETITORS

Gaining market share from a competitor is usually the hardest way to grow. Not only will your competitor fight to retain their customers but you have to show overwhelming reasons why customers should make the effort to switch to you. Make certain you know what you're doing when you make serious attempts to raid your competitor's customer base and increase your own market share.

In industries where everyone has just about the same operating model, market share wars are rarely fought because everyone realizes there will be no real winners. If everyone has pretty much the same costs, the only way to win market share is by reducing profits – which is neither rational nor sustainable. Growing by increasing your market share, therefore, centers around finding a creative way to give your competitors a problem in customer base retention.

To increase your market share, there are really only two things you can do:

1. *Challenge your rivals by providing a superior product or greater service value.*

 In any market, an incumbent has three main advantages over its potential competitors:

 ° Better access to information about its customers.
 ° Greater economic clout with its current customers.
 ° An opportunity to exert greater influence.

 Any outsider aspiring to steal market share from an established company first needs to overcome the incumbent's advantages. Usually, that will take superior effort or insight on the part of the new market entrant. Or the newcomer may try and level the playing field by removing any switching costs which would be incurred, or perhaps by using some creativity.

 To make any gains in market share sustainable, however, the new or aspiring market entrant must deliver truly superior value to customers. This is typically in the form of:

 ° *Operational excellence* – being able to offer lower prices or greater levels of service through more efficient supply-chain integration.
 ° *Product leadership* – the latest technology being brought to market before anyone else has yet offered the next-generation features.
 ° *Customer intimacy* – offering customers a solution that solves all of their problems. (A good customer-intimacy oriented company will become highly

adept at stealing solutions from its smartest customers, sanitizing those solutions and then offering them to other customers).

Customer value is never static. The customer's expectations rise each year. That means if you (as a newcomer) plan on keeping the market share you win off established companies, you need to commit to improving your value proposition every year. Within a very short period, competitors will match your standards of performance. Unless you keep adding more value over time, you will have little to differentiate yourself. Smart companies work hard to improve the amount of customer value they deliver year after year at a faster rate than competitors can match.

2. *Buy market share by acquiring your competitors*. Historically, this has involved two general approaches:

° *Industry roll-ups* – where small mom-and-pop operations in a fragmented industry are acquired to create a large enterprise that will have better economies of scale.
° *Outright acquisitions* – where the acquiring company buys a rival, integrates its customer base into its own operation and ceases operating the company which has been acquired.

Roll-ups work okay at first, but once they have been going for a while, the management's attention is so focused on absorbing the new companies that it never actually delivers the promised economies of scale. In addition, there is always an irresistible temptation to pay for the acquired companies in stock, which has a way of depreciating because the remaining companies will start asking for a premium to be acquired. In short, the roll-up approach never works long-term.

Outright acquisitions make good sense whenever three conditions apply:

° There is no price premium that has to be paid for the new customers. That is, customers can be acquired for a net cost that genuinely reflects their future economic value to the company buying them.

° The operating model of the company making the acquisition must be sufficiently robust enough that the new customers can be integrated into the existing business processes – rather than needing different operating processes to be catered for.

° Management is in place which knows how to make acquisitions work quickly and effectively. The faster an acquisition can be integrated, the less clutter and bureaucracy that will develop.

"When a company uses cash that it has generated, from either earnings or borrowings, to make an acquisition, that organization is providing growth for every shareholder. But when a company issues more of its own stock to make an acquisition or sells stock to others to raise cash for an acquisition, it may very well not be providing growth for every shareholder.

After all, if two companies pool their interests and their shareholders to create one larger entity, is that growth? From a competitive perspective, yes, because the new entity has greater market share and presumably is a more formidable competitor. But from a shareholder perspective, all that has happened is that the pie has gotten bigger, but the investor's share has become proportionately smaller. That's why Warren Buffett is emphatic that his Berkshire Hathaway will not pay for acquisitions with new shares of Berkshire. Buffett likes to pay cash that he has generated from earnings."

– Michael Treacy

"Whichever strategy you choose to effect a market share gain, you should always be aware of the dangers of this discipline. Recognize that it's a lot easier to get hurt by a market share slide than it is to create a market share surge. And always consider the other parts of the growth portfolio, which may offer an easier and less costly way to grow. Generally speaking, companies don't lose market share so much as they are forced to yield it to a superior force. Their customers depart because competitors have stolen them away."

– Michael Treacy

GROWTH DISCIPLINE #3: POSITION YOURSELF WHERE GROWTH WILL HAPPEN

Establishing a presence in the fastest-growing segments of your market and ensuring you get a decent slice of the pie is usually the easiest way to grow. The major problems here are being able to spot emerging opportunities quickly enough and then securing sufficient market share as these markets become better defined. It's all about getting positioned early enough to take advantage.

If you can identify early enough where growth is going to happen in your market and get established there, it won't matter if your competitors dominate all the other segments. You will automatically outgrow them just on the strength of your own positioning. By shifting your market mix to invade the booming market segments, your business will grow rapidly. Unsurprisingly, the basic challenge of this growth discipline is to spot growing market segments early before your competitors can. To do this, you should organize your management team to pick up on the three leading indicators of emerging fast-growth markets:

1. *Shifts in consumer buying criteria*

   When customers change their preferred value demands, that can accelerate growth substantially in different segments. For example, when customers changed their preference in pickup trucks from price to design around 1994, this market segment enjoyed a renaissance.

2. ***Innovations generating leaps in customer value***
   Whenever customer value rises dramatically in a market segment, all those on the fringes will rush in enthusiastically. This increase in value may be generated by:

   ° Technology breakthroughs or other advances.
   ° Business process enhancements.
   ° The introduction of outside expertise.
   ° The adoption of a new business model.

   Most frequently, leaps in customer value arise when an operating model which has been very successful in another industry is transferred successfully to your market. When the new operating model is coupled with innovative technology or process upgrades, the leap in customer value can be notably large – generating sizeable demand for growth.

3. ***General demographic trends***
   If a large number of people experience a major change in their lifestyle, you should pay close attention because these types of changes always create impressive market-positioning opportunities. These changes are generally the result of:

   ° Large groups moving into different life stages.
   ° The ebbs and flows of migration patterns.
   ° The availability of new employment opportunities.

   One notable factor about demographic trends is their

predictability. For example, the baby-boomer generation has caused numerous economic booms and busts as it has progressed through the various life stages. Forecasting which products and services will be demanded by this group in the future is very obvious. All you need do is forecast what the economic impact will be on your industry and position your own business enterprise in some of the fastest growing segments.

So if market-positioning is the easiest way to grow, why do so few companies do this well? The main reason is comparatively few organizations take a systematic approach to spotting emerging opportunities and taking advantage of them. Most businesses tend to get so caught up in operational matters they give little thought or attention to repositioning opportunities.

Smart companies make spotting new high growth markets a continuing focus of management. Ideally, turning up new and promising market positions should receive as much attention as is devoted to ongoing attempts to reduce costs. Plus, business managers need to become students of their entire market and not just the niche they currently occupy. This is a rare situation where the benefits of the broad view substantially outweigh the advantages of focus. Emerging market opportunities will need to be pieced together from a variety of sources.

If you don't understand the dynamics of every segment within your market, if you can't at any moment accurately predict the potential for growth in total gross profits for all of these segments, then you become a prisoner of your own ignorance. Lacking well-understood options, you cannot take advantage of the repositioning possibilities. Much of the data required to reach that informed state will not be generated by your financial-reporting systems, and it usually can't be bought from a syndicated data service. It has to be pieced together using research, private and public information sources, and analytic detective work. Create an information base that encompasses past and current shifts in buying criteria, value innovation and demographics. Gauge market segment size as well as current and forecast growth rates. It's a considerable task, but it can be done with a commitment of time and talent.

– Michael Treacy

Sometimes, your analysis will lead you to conclude market repositioning just won't help – the dynamics of your industry are miserable and have always been that way. It may be many years since anyone in your industry generated a decent return on their capital invested, and no emerging growth market segments are available. In that case, you really have just three options:

1. *Sell out* – and put your capital into an emerging market segment in another industry.
2. *Restructure your industry* – by buying your competitors and closing them down to reduce overcapacity.
3. *Use some ingenuity* – and create a next-generation business model that exploits a problem nobody else has ever noticed.

> *"The good news is that, for the vast majority of businesses, the growth that comes with market positioning does not require such heroic efforts. You do need to have a firm comprehension of your market segments, and a weather eye on the signals that are or may soon be changing – the shifts in customer criteria, customer value, and demographics. The chances are good that the effort you make to follow this third discipline of market growth will be well rewarded."*
>
> – Michael Treacy

> *"When you make your move into a growing market segment, you should invade in force. It's a no-brainer: the stronger your position in a booming market segment, the larger your gain. If you have zero percent of a segment growing at 100-percent a year, you get zero. If you can get in on the ground floor and build a decent position, then 100-percent market growth will automatically double your business every year."*
>
> – Michael Treacy

GROWTH DISCIPLINE #4: INVADE YOUR ADJACENT MARKETS

To do this well, you need an ability to accurately appraise what your core operating capabilities are and how they could be applied advantageously in an ancillary market. Once you know those factors, it then comes down to a simple build vs. acquire decision – do you build your own operational capabilities in that new segment or acquire them from someone else?

Every market has its own distinctive set of:

- Cost structures
- Competitors
- Customers
- Operational capabilities

If there are no variations in these four factors, there is just the one market. If there are small variations in the criteria, then you have different segments within the same market. If there are important similarities as well as large differences, then you have an adjacent market. For example, the video games market is adjacent to the consumer electronics business – there are enough differences to make it a separate market but enough similarities to make it familiar.

Any company contemplating a move into an adjacent market needs to find the answer to three key questions:

1. *Does this market offer enough opportunities for growth and profitability to make entering it worthwhile?*

   That is, do the potential benefits make it worth our time and effort? If the adjacent market is stable, the entrenched competitors won't give up without a fight. Most likely, they will sacrifice some short-term profitability in order to keep competitors out. You first need to determine whether the market is large enough to make fighting for it worthwhile.

   Quite often, this factor is difficult to assess. Ideally, you want to enter an adjacent market when it's in a state of flux. You also have the problem that as an outsider looking in, your knowledge is theoretical. The entrenched competitors have hard-earned experience with the realities of the situation. They know better than you do how large the adjacent market will grow. The best time to enter a market is when the incumbents are so busy fighting each other or adjusting to change they have less time and energy to devote to fighting new market entrants.

2. *If we entered this market, what would be our main competitive advantages?*

   Moving into an adjacent market only makes sense if you can bring to bear advantages that will make you the market leader. Keep in mind also you have to be able to execute. If your advantages are not tangible or practical, it's most unlikely you will prevail. Moving into an adjacent market on the basis of theoretical or visionary advantages almost guarantees you will be dead-on-arrival.

For example, AT&T paid top dollar to acquire cable companies. The vision was to deliver a single bundle of offerings including local, long-distance, wireless, Internet and cable TV. AT&T never managed to implement, however, and competitors flooded the markets with other offers. As a result, AT&T lost more than $150 billion of market value as investors, analysts and shareholders became more pessimistic about the company's future.

3. ***Can we match the standards of the existing and potential competitors in this market?***

Put differently, this means can you match the standards of quality which are already common in this market? To do that, you'll need to have in place three factors:

° Comparable technology to underpin the products or services you are planning on selling.
° Established relationships with suppliers and other industry stakeholders with whom you will need to partner.
° A business model which will create value for your customers, your investors and other key stakeholders.

As a rule-of-thumb, unless you have at least 80-percent of these factors in place, don't even contemplate entering an adjacent market.

If you can answer these three questions well, you then face a make-versus-buy decision about the best way to enter an adjacent market. That is, should you use your current resources and skills to carve out a market share or should you buy your way in? Both choices have advantages and disadvantages. The natural tendency is to prefer organic growth but that often means you miss important market nuances and relationships. On the other hand, acquiring a functioning company will get you up and running quickly, but integrating the acquisition into your own company over the long haul (which you have to do) usually proves to be more difficult than originally envisaged.

> *"If you're going to enter a dynamic adjacent market, you must time your entry carefully. Too early, and you throw away your resources on a market that won't ripen for years. Too late, and you have to cope with established, hostile incumbents."*
>
> *– Michael Treacy*

> *"One of the grand illusions of adjacency growth is that 'because I have a sophisticated business model, I can automatically apply it to an adjacent market and rout the incumbents'. Amazon.com made that assumption when it announced that it was applying its book selling model to all retail markets. The move failed, predictably, because retail markets have many varied characteristics, and a business model that works in one almost surely can't be applied to all of them. With-*

out the specific know-how concerning promotions, merchandise management, and logistics, and without key supplier and channel relationships, Amazon has had a tough time outside of books and music, Amazon's traditional markets. It has taken mountains of losses to convince Jeff Bezos, Amazon's founder, that his company cannot simply waltz into adjacent retail markets and take them over."

– Michael Treacy

"One familiar form of the dynamic market that attracts new entrants seeking adjacency growth occurs because of a generational shift in technology, process or customer value. Generational shifts are far from guaranteed opportunities, however. In general, companies do a mediocre job of analyzing the attractiveness of an adjacent market because they are outsiders looking in, without the hard-earned knowledge that has become almost instinctive to incumbents. Newcomers assess the possibilities on paper, rather than on the basis of experience."

– Michael Treacy

"Adjacent markets might seem like natural targets, but there are potential pitfalls on every side."

– Michael Treacy

GROWTH DISCIPLINE #5: CONSISTENTLY INVEST IN NEW LINES OF BUSINESS

This growth discipline is built on smart investment decisions rather than sound management skills. Most often, business management teams don't have significant skills in this area and therefore further training and experience will be required before pursuing this growth discipline.

Going into a whole new line of business in an entirely different industry is a high-risk growth strategy. Put simply, unless you know what you're doing and you have the human and financial resources to be able to execute, it's very easy to waste a lot of time and other resources without generating any significant growth. To win this way requires an investor's mind-set rather than the viewpoint of a manager.

What's the difference between investors and managers?

- Great managers are intensely passionate about the line of business they are in. They thrive on overcoming challenges, and love to learn about their products and markets in ever-finer detail. They have an optimistic, can-do approach to most challenges.
- Successful investors are objective above all. They keep personal sentiment out of their decisions. They are realists and cynics. A good investor will be prepared to pass up hundreds of investment opportunities before they find one they like.

Investors who succeed in making acquisitions work usually follow some rather straight-forward mandates:

- *Never overpay for a new line of business* – so if the price gets too high, walk away. There will always be another opportunity tomorrow, so don't feel like you've got to do a deal today. Good investors let logic rather than emotion guide their decisions. Therefore, irrespective of any other factors, if the numbers don't work out, investors are prepared to walk away and look for another deal.
- *Keep it simple* – because the more complex a strategy the business has, the less likely it will be able to execute. Watch out for business and markets where steady and practical improvements in operations will increase sales and profits in the future. Those businesses are the ones to buy. Don't look for businesses where dramatic breakthroughs will be required before the industry becomes profitable. You may not be able to wait long enough for the anticipated results to actually materialize.
- *Partner with the management team of the company you acquire* – and make it worth their while to move forward. Investors don't want to run the business, they want to grow the business. Therefore, investors spend as much time evaluating management teams as they do deciding whether or not to invest in a business. They work on the basis that a good acquisition is really a partnership with the management team of the com-

pany being acquired. If the management team don't like the idea of working in tandem with the new owners to grow the business, investors look elsewhere.

As a general approach, most investors tend to make small acquisitions in an industry first before attempting to make a major acquisition. That way they get a feel for the real-world issues involved before committing serious money. It also gives them a better feel for the questions they should be asking when analyzing whether or not to make other acquisitions in the future. This approach lowers the risk level and enhances the manageability factor.

Companies that grow successfully by moving into new lines of business tend to have three essential core capabilities:

1. *They are good at scanning the horizon and identifying the right market and the right acquisition targets in that market.*
   Naturally, the right market in this context is a high-growth emerging market. In this environment, all the participants are likely to prosper. Once a good market has been found, the key questions then become centered around finding the right company to acquire. Investors look at three factors:

   ° *The company's positioning* – what its current cash flow is, whether it is targeting high-growth niches, how it is positioned for the future.
   ° *The quality of the management team* – whether they

can adjust to changing circumstances and so forth.

° *The company's strategic plan* – whether it is simple enough and practical enough to be achievable. If the plan calls for "transforming markets" or "making breakthroughs in customer value", beware. Those concepts are easy to talk about but difficult to deliver.

2. *They are experienced and competent at valuing and structuring good acquisition deals.*

Too many companies pay premium prices for their acquisitions. This happens when decisions are driven by management aspirations rather than marketplace realities. Invariably, future synergies get mentioned as the rationale for paying a premium price, but these tend to be illusory in nature. Savvy investors use "earnouts" – where the purchase price is contingent on future performance and convertible debt instruments or preferred shares are used to place the purchaser first in line should the acquisition transaction need to be unwound in the future. Structuring a good deal is an art form in and of itself.

3. *They are willing to exert financial, managerial and strategic control over the acquired businesses.*

It's important that the new line of business stand on its own rather than be cross-subsidized from elsewhere. Therefore, the new company should be operated as an independent business unit, but its management needs to be integrated into the parent corporation. In practice, this means providing the management team with the correct incentives.

> "Deal making beats working. Deal making is exciting and fun, and working is grubby. Running anything is primarily an enormous amount of grubby detail work. Deal making is romantic, sexy. That's why you have deals that make no sense."
>
> – Peter Drucker

> "Don't get carried away. Be skeptical about that apparent adjacency, and when a sexy deal beckons, take a cold shower. Above all, take off your manager's rose-colored glasses and peer through the clear lens of an investor whenever you see anything even remotely like a new market. And when you spot an opportunity, take a deep breath, and try it on for size."
>
> – Michael Treacy

> "Most efforts to diversify into unrelated businesses are unsuccessful, and most managers are poor investors outside their core markets."
>
> – Michael Treacy

BALANCE: HAVE A BALANCED PORTFOLIO WHICH CONTAINS GROWTH INITIATIVES IN ALL FIVE DISCIPLINES

In just the same way as a venture capitalist has a portfolio of investments – some of which will bomb while others become superstars – business managers need a portfolio of growth initiatives under way at any one time. That way if one or two of these areas fail to perform, the other growth initiatives can still deliver. This is the essence of risk management and the key to consistent double-digit growth.

Each of the five growth disciplines require different skill sets to pull them off, but there is one factor which is consistent right across the spectrum – uncertainty. To be more specific, despite your best intentions and efforts, some of these growth strategies will work and others will not. Even the most astute of plans can be derailed by a piece of bad luck completely outside your sphere of influence. And therefore, you have to spread your bets rather than relying on just one or two of these strategies to work out as planned.

All the growth strategies face four main risks:

1. *Demand risk* – the level of consumer demand for your product or service. Customers always want more for their money all the time. In some industries (like fashion), the demand risk will be high. In others, demand risk is almost nonexistent.
2. *Competitor risk* – what others in the marketplace will be willing to do to win new customers. Again, this varies widely from one industry to the next, and will also be dependent on the introduction of new technology and how that changes the market dynamics.
3. *Implementation risk* – how effectively a business enterprise turns its intentions into action. Even if the company accurately forecasts demand and anticipates customer moves, things can still go wrong. Quite often, implementation risk is the greatest of all four types of risk. The most successful businesses tend to be those that narrow their focus and concentrate on doing selective things well rather than attempting to be everything to everyone.
4. *Operating risk* – logistics failures, service breakdowns and manufacturing problems. Even when a business has implemented well, there is still the danger product or service breakdowns at the consumer level will impede operations and drive customers to competitors. The higher the performance expectations that are created, the greater the opportunities for operating risks to eventuate.

Smart companies don't follow one or two of the growth initiatives and hope for the best. Instead, they put together a balanced portfolio of separate growth initiatives. This is done by selecting the growth tactics most likely to succeed, balancing the optimum selection against management goals and then allowing for rational marketplace and execution constraints. This is very similar in concept to the way a venture capitalist works. A successful venture capitalist allocates capital and other resources across a portfolio of investment opportunities. The venture capitalist then works with each investment to add whatever is needed for it to succeed. However, venture capitalists are, above all, realists. If an investment fails, it is quickly dropped from the portfolio so as not to impact on the other investments.

In order for this balanced portfolio approach to work for growth initiatives, constant attention must be paid to four major areas:

1. *The portfolio must be adapted to meet changing conditions.* In just the same was as astute investors skew their portfolios depending on current market conditions, managers of growth portfolios need to do the same. Growth initiatives need to be regularly fine-tuned to target emerging growth markets. When markets slow down, growth initiatives that target adjacent markets should come to the fore. In other words, the portfolio should be fine-tuned to meet the market rather than hoping the market will come to you. Note

also this growth portfolio approach is not about fundamental transformations of the business – like abandoning your established business lines and moving to the New Economy. That is a high-risk strategy which works rarely and makes no sense except in exceptional circumstances.

2. *The portfolio must be sufficiently diversified to reduce risk.* Instead of trying to generate double-digit growth through one or two initiatives alone, smart managers have active growth initiatives in all five disciplines which are complementary and coordinated. That way, the moves of a wily competitor, unanticipated execution problems or simply a hitch or delay in any one of these initiatives won't derail overall growth. In addition, the five growth disciplines complement each other. That way growth is delivered by steady one-step-at-a-time actions rather than making high-risk bet-your-company attempts.

3. *The portfolio will require a high level of management talent.* This is the key distinction between an investment portfolio and a growth portfolio. With an investment portfolio, once you buy a stock, there's nothing else to do. Your returns will be dependent on the skill of distant managers. With a growth portfolio of initiatives, however, the growth achieved will be heavily dependent on your own company's managers. How your managers respond to the actions of competitors, to changes

in customer preferences and to unanticipated factors will determine whether your growth goals are realized or not. This is good – it puts you in the driver's seat.

4. *A robust and comprehensive growth information management system must be in place.*

Most organizations have a management system in place for controlling financial performance. A parallel system is needed for managing growth built around accurate, detailed and timely information. Data needs to be broken down so there is clarification about how much growth is actually being achieved in specific markets as a result of the various initiatives. At the very minimum, a growth reconciliation statement is needed so you can tell:

- ° What the growth rate is in each market segment.
- ° What your market share is in each segment.
- ° The weighting of your various growth initiatives.
- ° The amount of churn (customer turnover) in each segment.
- ° The gains in growth achieved in each segment.
- ° The number of new customers doing business with you.

Once you are gathering this information on a regular basis, you can then set specific targets in each growth initiative for the managers to work towards. You can also delegate responsibility and authority as seems wise. For example, business unit leaders may become responsible not only for meeting their usual targets but also for realizing their growth objectives. This way everyone gets committed to achieving double-digit growth.

Keep in mind also that business growth itself is a self-reinforcing process that builds on past growth performance. The more a company grows, the easier it becomes for the company to keep growing in the future. Growth in business is driven by three virtuous cycles that act as catalysts for future growth:

- Virtuous Growth Cycle #1 – Economic
  Faster growth always leads to higher price/earnings multiples, which in turn lead to a higher share price. The higher the share price is, the easier it becomes for a company to raise capital (through borrowing or issuing new shares). The more capital an enterprise has, the greater the investment it will make, which will in turn drive more growth in the future.
- Virtuous Growth Cycle #2 – Momentum
  Fast growth always attracts the attention of customers and enhances the company's reputation for excellence. Greater customer confidence, in turn, means more new customers will want to do business in the future which will result in still more growth as the cycle repeats.
- Virtuous Growth Cycle #3 – Opportunity
  Growth always generates more internal opportunities for people to get promoted, which increases morale. High morale means the staff will be eager to innovate and improve their productivity, which subsequently will

lead to better customer value. And the better and more attractive the company's value proposition is, the more customers will sign on in the future.

Therefore, smart corporate managers will make sure their businesses are growing consistently. To do otherwise is to choose to fail, especially in a competitive marketplace where others are working hard to harness the dynamics of the virtuous cycles of growth to their own advantage.

"Double-digit growth doesn't come free. A business doesn't grow because the economy permits it, the government subsidizes it, customers clamor for it, or a higher power shines its light upon it. In fact, hardly any of the forces you contend with really want you to grow, since your gain portends their loss. Yet double-digit growth is not a dream but a plausible scenario. The economy, though important, is but a small factor in the growth potential of any one company. Competition, though fierce, can be outfought and outflanked. Customers, though demanding, want to grow with value-creating suppliers."

– Michael Treacy

"What is my yardstick for growth? Revenue and net profit growth are useful measures, but, in my view, they work best as a supplement to another number – gross profits – that is, revenues minus the direct cost

of the goods or services being sold. Gross profits are a direct measure of the value that a company creates for its customers. Subtract from revenue all the costs of raw materials, labor, and other production costs, and what you have is a measure of the value that a company has added to the product above and beyond its material and labor content. That's the true measure of market size, and a gain in gross profits is the truest measure of growth. Gross profit numbers eliminate whatever costs and benefits the customer doesn't consider relevant. And, in that light, the annual increase or decrease in a company's gross profit is the best gauge for managers to use internally in determining how their companies are faring and growing in their markets."

– Michael Treacy

"The central thesis – that any business can achieve steady double-digit growth – isn't for everyone. After all, there isn't enough growth in our economy for every company to achieve double-digit growth. But your organization can achieve it, even if others can't."

– Michael Treacy

"When I began gathering data more than five years ago, my hypothesis was that the difference between steady fast-growth businesses and also-rans would be found in their strategy. Growth companies must

be making different decisions, placing different bets, and building better strategies than everyone else, I thought. As the research progressed, however, and more data were gathered and analyzed, what became clear was that the major difference was that high-growth firms approached the challenge of growth in a more sophisticated way. They built robust portfolios of growth initiatives that spread risk and improved the predictability of results. Further, they employed sophisticated management systems for planning, controlling and measuring growth that were different from other organizations in the study. In slower or unsteady growth firms, growth management was a much more haphazard process. Steady double-digit growth was the result of a comprehensive system for managing growth as a portfolio of opportunities and initiatives. Any firm can adopt this system for managing a growth portfolio and achieve steady double-digit growth."

– Michael Treacy

"Right now, growth management in many organizations is almost laughable. Ask nearly any management team to meet a cost budget, cut 10-percent from its expenses, or implement a new process improvement, and it is generally up to the task. That's because the techniques for achieving those results are well understood. But ask the same managers to grow *at double-digit rates, and they typically look blank. They clearly lack the tools – the disciplines – to tackle growth in a structured, systematic way. Too many management teams view double-digit growth as something beyond their control – a sudden change in customer taste, say, or an unexpected breakthrough in their research labs. They assume it's all in the lap of the gods, like winning the lottery. They have no idea that it is the result of disciplined management practices."*

– Michael Treacy

"For many businesses, single-digit growth has become the norm. Why do so many managers accept low growth? Is it because they secretly love the status quo and are afraid of change? Growth, after all, rivals profit as the most sacred word in the business canon. No, this contagion of dither and drift is more likely caused by ignorance than by fear."

– Michael Treacy

"'Growth is the only evidence of life,' wrote John Henry Newman, the great nineteenth-century English writer and Catholic cardinal. Precisely the same rule applies to companies: growth is the only hope of true business success. Double-digit growth is a realistic and attainable business goal. Quite simply, it can be achieved by thoroughly mastering and aggressively pursuing the

five disciplines that make up the growth portfolio. The target is visible. The tools are available. The payoff is enormous. The rest is up to you."

– Michael Treacy

Made in the USA
Monee, IL
11 July 2021

73329729R00026